Elements

THE CHESHIRE PRIZE FOR LITERATURE ANTHOLOGIES

Prize Flights: Stories from the Cheshire Prize for Literature 2003; edited by Ashley Chantler

Life Lines: Poems from the Cheshire Prize for Literature 2004; edited by Ashley Chantler

Word Weaving: Stories and Poems for Children from the Cheshire Prize for Literature 2005; edited by Jaki Brien

Edge Words: Stories from the Cheshire Prize for Literature 2006; edited by Peter Blair

Elements

Poems from the Cheshire Prize
for Literature
2007

Edited by Peter Blair

Chester Academic Press

First published 2008
by Chester Academic Press
Corporate Communications
University of Chester
Parkgate Road
Chester CH1 4BJ

Printed and bound in the UK by the
LIS Print Unit,
University of Chester
Cover designed by the
LIS Graphics Team,
University of Chester

A catalogue record for this book is available from
the British Library

For Bill Hughes

CONTENTS

vii

THE CONTRIBUTORS

Barbara Bentley lives in Croft, Warrington, and works as an English teacher and Divisional Manager at St John Rigby College, Orrell. Now that her two children have left the nest, she has more time to indulge her hobbies of reading, gardening, and writing. Her collection of poetry, *Living Next to Leda*, was published by Seren in 1996, after she gained an MA in Writing from the University of Glamorgan. Her poems and reviews have been published in various magazines, and she is currently assembling a manuscript of her recent work.

Tonia Bevins was born in Blackpool but has lived in Cheshire for nearly 30 years. After taking a degree in English and American Literature at the University of Manchester, she worked in broadcasting and as an ESOL teacher. She belongs to Vale Royal Writers' Group. One of her poems was published in *Life Lines: Poems from the Cheshire Prize for Literature 2004*.

Rob Blaney is 55 years old and works full-time as a Housing Manager for a Housing Association. He enjoys writing poetry on political and historical themes, and has been published in journals including *Agenda*, *Raw Edge*, *The New Writer*, and *Envoi*. He has completed a novel about suffragettes, and is currently writing a novel set during the 1930s.

Peter Branson organises workshops and literary events for various adult education bodies, and recently spent three years as Writer-in-Residence for the "All Write" project at Stoke-on-Trent Central Library. He has had poems published in many journals, including *Ambit*, *Fire*, *14*,

Other Poetry, Poetry Nottingham, Pulsar, South, and *The Interpreter's House;* five poems were included in the summer 2006 edition of *Envoi,* and he appeared in *Acumen* for the second time in January 2008. He also had a poem published in *Life Lines.* In 2006 he received a "highly commended" award in the Petra Kenny Poetry Competition and won first prize in the October *Envoi* International Poetry Competition. Last year he was runner-up in the *Writing Magazine* Open Poetry Competition.

Angi Holden is a mature student at MMU Cheshire, studying Creative Writing and finding university far more fun the second time around. While her course includes script and media, her particular interests are poetry and the short story, and much of her writing explores identity, often in the context of family relationships. A keen reader, she is involved with an adult reading group at her local library and a teenage reading group at her local high school.

George Horsman retired early from university teaching and lives in Chester. He has had many poems and several short stories published or broadcast on regional radio, and has achieved some success in local competitions, being twice short-listed for his short stories and winning two awards for poetry. He also had a poem included in *Life Lines.* His other interests include hillwalking, choral singing, and learning German.

Gill McEvoy is a widely published poet who runs three local poetry events: the Golden Pear Poetry Reading Group; the Poem Shed (a monthly poetry workshop); and ZEST! (a bimonthly Open Floor Poetry Evening at

Alexander's Jazz Theatre Bar, Rufus Court, Chester). Two of Gill's poems featured in *Life Lines*, and a pamphlet entitled *Uncertain Days* was published by Happenstance Press in 2006. Her second collection is in the pipeline.

Clive McWilliam has worked throughout Britain and abroad as a landscape architect and illustrator, and has his own practice in Chester. He had a poem included in *Life Lines*, and last year was runner-up in the Cheshire Prize for a short story, which was published in *Edge Words: Stories from the Cheshire Prize for Literature 2006*. When not working, he also likes painting, walking, and middle-distance staring. He is married with three children, and has lived in Chester for 24 years.

Rita Ray lives in Lymm, Cheshire, and is a member of Six Poets (www.sixpoets.org.uk), a group that meets for workshops and occasional readings. She has had poems published in magazines and journals, and her stories and poems for children have appeared in several anthologies. Rita also enjoys painting portraits and seascapes, and finds art a rich source of ideas for poems. She takes paints and sketchbook whenever she travels, and has been particularly inspired by trips to remote areas of China.

Andrew Rudd has lived in Cheshire for more than 30 years, and was Cheshire Poet Laureate for 2006. His poems have appeared in all kinds of places: magazines, bookmarks, postcards, library windows, on stage, in prison, and on radio. His first collection, *One Cloud Away from the Sky*, was published in 2007. In his "day job" he is Senior Lecturer at Manchester Metropolitan University. Andrew also won the Cheshire Prize for Literature in 2004 and his winning poems were published in *Life Lines*.

Frances Sackett was born in rural Wales and lives in Marple. She is a member of Marple Writers, and for six years has led a Poetry Appreciation class for Continuing Education at the University of Manchester. Landscape has always figured extensively in her poems, as has the plight of women, especially in war-stricken countries. She is widely published in journals and anthologies, including *Parents* (Enitharmon), *Childhood* and *Birdsong* (both Seren), and recently *Poems For Peace* (United Nations Association). She also had a poem in *Life Lines*. Her collection *The Hand Glass* is published by Seren.

Ruth A. Symes (www.ruthasymes.com) was born in Warrington and lives in Altrincham. Having been an academic, teacher, and editor, she now freelances for a variety of family history and literary magazines. Other recent writing projects have included editing the memoirs of a Cheshire farmer and producing her own book on family history. Ruth is also editor of *The Memoirs* (the journal of the Manchester Literary and Philosophical Society) and *Portico Quarterly* (the newsletter of the Portico Library, Manchester). One of her poems was published in *Life Lines*.

Angela Topping has lived in Cheshire all her life and teaches English at Upton Hall, a grammar school on the Wirral. Her first work of literary criticism, on Michael Frayn's novel *Spies*, has just been published by Greenwich Exchange. She is also an experienced teacher of Creative Writing, and has edited two anthologies. Angela's own poetry, both for adults and for children, has been widely published, and one of her poems appeared in *Life Lines*. She has produced three collections, including a New and

Selected entitled *The Fiddle* (Stride) and, most recently, *The Way We Came* (Bluechrome).

Joy Winkler was born in Barnsley, but has lived in Macclesfield for 19 years. A lot of her poetry has been inspired by the towns and people she has known. One of her poems appeared in *Life Lines*, and she has had three collections published: *Morag's Garden*, *Built to Last*, and *On the Edge*. Joy is Writer-in-Residence at Styal Prison, and was Cheshire Poet Laureate for 2005.

Stephen Wrigley, a Wirral poet in his early 60s, has written poetry since childhood. In recent years he has produced five collections (one illustrated), featured in magazines and pamphlets, and enjoyed some success in competitions. His poetry has also been read on BBC Radio Merseyside arts programmes. In his view, poetry should be understandable rather than obscure, reflect common life experiences, and give enjoyment to the reader or listener. He helps run the Greasby Poetry Society, which meets monthly in the library there.

Peter Blair (editor) is Senior Lecturer in English at the University of Chester, where he specialises in twentieth-century literature, colonial and postcolonial literature, and creative writing. He was formerly an editor with a publishing company, and has made numerous contributions to major reference books. Peter's poems and stories have appeared in periodicals and anthologies, and he has been short-listed and runner-up in the short-story section of the Bridport Prize. He has published articles and reviews on various aspects of South African literature, and is currently writing a book on the liberal tradition in the South African novel. He is co-editor with Ashley

Chantler of *Flash: The International Short-Short Story Magazine* (www.chester.ac.uk/flash.magazine).

FOREWORD

"My favourite poem is the one that starts 'Thirty days hath September' because it actually tells you something" (Groucho Marx). The poems comprising this collection, the fifth to arise from the annual Cheshire Prize for Literature, are the best of the many, many entries we received. Each poet has placed "the *best* words in the best order" (Coleridge), and refrained from telling us anything banal, rather shown us a glimpse of a complex, sometimes troubling, sometimes wonderful, world.

The overall winner was Andrew Rudd for "Instructions for a Maths Lesson", "Moldoviţa Monastery", "A Turkish Miniature", and "Dead Face". The two runners-up were (in alphabetical order): Clive McWilliam, for "Young Seal I Found", "Stuffed Pike and Young Flora", "Blind Faith", "Harvest", and "Unearthed"; and Stephen Wrigley, for "The Roundabout", "The Windhover", "Decorator", "Pierhead, December", and "Celebration".

I must thank my fellow judges – Peter Blair (University of Chester) and John Scrivener (Deputy Chairman of the Chester Literature Festival) – for their hard work and judiciousness, and our guest judge, the Poet Laureate Andrew Motion, for his support of the judging panel and entertaining talk at the prize-giving evening. That evening was made even more memorable by my colleague Derek Alsop, who spoke with good humour about writing poetry.

Thanks are also due to Lynda Baguley for her perfect organising of the competition and the prize-giving evening; Peter Blair for his scrupulous editing; Peter Williams for publishing and working on the collection; and Diane Dennis for the cover design. I am also sincerely grateful for the help of other colleagues and associates of the Department of English, especially Linden Alsop,

Melissa Fegan, Francesca Haig, Sarah Heaton, Emma Rees, Yvonne Siddle, and William Stephenson.

The competition continued to be sponsored generously by the Bank of America and administered by the University of Chester's Corporate Communications Department.

In 2008, the Cheshire Prize for Literature will be for writing for children, and we hope to publish a selection of the best entries, including the prizewinners, in the equivalent volume next year.

This volume is dedicated to Bill Hughes, who did so much to ensure the success of the Cheshire Prize for Literature in its first four years.

Ashley Chantler
Chair, Judging Panel
Department of English
University of Chester
30th December 2007

Andrew Rudd

INSTRUCTIONS FOR A MATHS LESSON

Entwine your right ankle
round the right chair leg.
Twist the chair back, jostle it
     up and down.

Advance your pencil
slowly across the table
by blowing. Stretch your sweatshirt
up over your mouth and nose. Bend
the blue ruler across your face
     side to side.

Yawn cavernously.

Pull your hair into a tight bunch,
twist slowly. Lean in across the table
until your centre of gravity is well forward
then push your chair with the back of your calf
     to and fro.

Sit with your right leg crossed
underneath you so that the foot
catches the table leg and allows
the chair to pivot
     back and forth.

When you absolutely have to,
write down the numbers,
add them.

Andrew Rudd

MOLDOVIȚA MONASTERY

In fresco blue
     torn from Bucovina sky

Father and Son preside over
     the end of time; below them

the Holy Dove perches
     on the shining book, on a cloth

draped across the Judgement Throne –
     on which irreplaceable blue

in 1868, an Austrian soldier
     balanced on a ladder

scratches the paint to write
     in confident copperplate

       Mathilde.

At dusk he brings her to see
     what he's written. She cranes

her neck, looks up, laughs. He slides
     his hand around her

white skin
     among blackened icons,

smouldering prayer stools:
     the echo of her cry.

And now, nearer than ever
    to the end of time:

Look! says the tourist – *that pigeon,*
    it's called Mathilde!

Andrew Rudd

A TURKISH MINIATURE

Wiry dogs
    snapping,
        slinking
            scrawny-bellied
dodge round
    the edge
        of a shining
            circle where
the sword-swallower
    luridly lighting
        his thrust-out
            chin, holds them
spellbound –
    the street men,
        the red-hats,
            the women
almost tumbling
    from balconies
        in a breathless
            moment before
hungry clouds
    swallow
        the golden
            sharpened
moon.

Andrew Rudd

DEAD FACE

She lies on the pew beside him, dead face
in a heart-shaped frame. Years pass, but his tie
is still black, his suit funereal. Going to kneel
at the rail, she seems to rest in his hand

gazing up at the priest. Back in his place
he mumbles to this personal saint. And I think, why
make such a show? Isn't it private, what you feel,
not a public performance? I don't understand

how you can speak to a snap, or fondly embrace
brass. It's a way, I suppose, of not saying goodbye.
No rules apply, there's no brake for the wheel
of grief. Her grip, her glance, a single strand

between you and all that would spring apart
if you once let slip the coils of your tensile heart.

Clive McWilliam

YOUNG SEAL I FOUND

as still as warmed rock,
in an inlet of bare-headed stones;

I almost broke his salty glaze –
and relived the rubbery give underfoot.

Whether washed-up or basking, I took his back legs,
startled at his dog-dense weight,

the curl and snap of him at arm's length,
as we struggle to the sea.

His mother, like a Russian doll,
bobs three waves away –

my involuntary grunt as I lob him
bounces round the bay.

The two of us watch as he hits the sea,
and turn as he raises the tide.

Clive McWilliam

STUFFED PIKE AND YOUNG FLORA

Boat Inn, Erbistock

Our clothes full of water,
we wait by the fire to dry,
where my rained-in daughter
is caught by his glare on the wall.

Later, outside, her appetite gone,
I show her the darkness he came from.
Lean into the surface that probably dropped
an inch or two the moment he left.

There must be a print in the weeds,
a mark down there where he'd been all that time,
so still and a part of the mud,
where eddies couldn't move him,

before the line, drawn like a wire
from the river, a shiver in the hands
heaving him out – dazzled, snagged,
like a stocking filled with sand.

I watch her living this. Her mouth moves,
trying to recapture the shock he would feel:
his gawp through the glare, the cast of that eye,
pulled out of darkness to the other side.

Clive McWilliam

BLIND FAITH

A boy at midday hides beneath his coat,
peers through the weave and buttonholes the sky.
And down the streets the dazzled hundreds, hoping
for epiphany through scraps of darkened glass,
are distilling drops of sunlight down a telescope.
Above, the fizzing of a tiny planet,
waiting for the clouds to pass.
And the day holds its breath by the side of the road
for pinhole Venus, slipping between
in her heliotropic trance.
United in this rare alignment,
each of us scorched and a part of the sky.
In blinding light, eight minutes to reach us,
an astronomical speck in the eye.

Clive McWilliam

HARVEST

In a young summer
he fell down between haystacks.
In the scythe of sky
he thought of the last sheaf
and the eye of the waiting hare.

Clive McWilliam

UNEARTHED

They showed me an open sack –
like a hole in the ground, with something cold
folded in the gamey dark;
something raw they'd pulled from a field,
now held limp by its ears it fills the room,

this puppet with a bullet in its side,
firelight flashing in a half-lidded eye
might warm and wake and send him round
the room – scratching, soily, scattering the fire,
unmaking beds, looking for the moon.

Stephen Wrigley

THE ROUNDABOUT

At the roundabout, when you miss third gear
and stall, I flinch. The jolt is harsh, abrupt
not just in journeying but at the here,
the now. Our visit's brevity seems stuffed
into this stop and, whilst there is no crash,
we feel the wrench of separation, loss,
of distances compacted in one flash
of fear. You wake, you tell me now, across
the dying night's transition into dawn
at four or five, recalling all the words
and fondness shared, against the morning's crawl
from dark to light towards the waking birds.
Before we dared to talk or chance a smile,
after the roundabout, we drove for miles.

Stephen Wrigley

THE WINDHOVER

after Gerard Manley Hopkins

A kestrel has come. In remorseless
narrative of wind and bird and sky,
he is the dark apostrophe of air,
the high question that moves, that does not,
the sudden slash of exclamation mark
that signifies his purpose, his intent.

Anchored in autumn, I put spade aside,
flex backwards, arch and oh, wish Hopkins
had not hijacked all the best of words.
Yet my spirit too like his can rise,
there beyond the tree line to the bird,
accompany a glide, share beat of wing,
tumble off the hover-point, plummet,
triumph at *the mastery of the thing.*

Stephen Wrigley

DECORATOR

The decorator's pots are full of paint
and repartee, and each invasive quip
he makes thins the emulsion of restraint
until all brushstrokes threaten runs or drips.
We're in the spare room, weeping at the mess,
his slapdash daybreak entrance to the house.
The chaos of our lives adds to the press.
You'd think he'd see, but this man has no nous.
Should I reveal my sentiments about
magnolia, brilliant white? I quite despair.
Every word he speaks sounds like a shout.
Those bare-board squeaks are deafening on the stair.
Ann, reinstate our bed, lay out the sheet.
I need to hear you breathe and touch your feet.

Stephen Wrigley

PIERHEAD, DECEMBER

Winter surges in. Storms overwhelm
the river reaches, fling protesting spray
vertical up shocked revetments.

Scarce conscious of the roar, I swim
in warm cocoon of pool, concentrate
on rhythm, rite of water passage,
imagining that I am music,
bars of Bach, his continuum of tune,
as near indifferent to pause as he.

Outside, wind flattens happiness
with North Atlantic force. Except –
the briefest lull – I see December sun
strike St Nicholas' with sudden light
and mint its clipper weathervane in gold.

Stephen Wrigley

CELEBRATION

Snow in February. Wet roads.
A service. My offer of an arm
is taken up. We find it droll
to be thought a pair. Little harm
in that, for friends of many years
who come to celebrate a life.
Remembrance, on a cold day, cheers
us, temporary husband, wife.

You ask me if I go to church.
I answer, "Yes, but just to pray."
A flower rota is as much
as you allow. Our lack of faith.
Yet friendship has its merits, no?
More firm than February snow.

Angi Holden

NICOSIA AIRPORT, JUNE '62

Tarmac softens, sticking to the soles
of my best sandals. An announcer's voice
apologises for the delay. Mother settles
in the square of shade, shakes out
her lace handkerchief, dabs her top lip.
A blush of powder blooms on white cotton,
a scarlet kiss caught on the border.
Father rattles towards us with a tray of tall glasses,
ice bouncing in the bubbles.
"Not long now," he says. And I stare
through the mirage into middle distance,
hold my breath, listen for the rumble of jet engines.
My sister is coming home for the holidays.

You remember it differently, of course.
The cramped aircraft cabin, the hours
folded into scratchy seats.
A parcel despatched from an overcast
June afternoon, with the promise of rain.
An airmail delivery, BFPO 53.
A summer feeling like a guest in your own home,
sunburn and prickly heat and expectations
piled up like the books left beside your dormitory bed,
the empty windows gazing across Essex fields.

Angi Holden

SALT

1. NaCl

Na. Sodium. Yellow.
The flicker of street lamps.
Cl. Chlorine. Green.
The scent of swimming pools.
NaCl. Sodium Chloride.
Elemental colours become compound white.

2. Salare

He turns the payslip in his hand.
Where does it all go?
Salary. *Salare.* Salt.
Footsteps of Roman legionaries
pound through his accounts;
cash slips like ground crystal
through his fingers.

3. The Mines

One hundred and seventy metres,
One hundred and seventy million years.
Beneath the Cheshire plain
trucks lumber through velvet-black galleries.
Excavate.
Above ground, salt heaps crust ochre.

4. Beans

Kilner jars.
A handful of runner beans,
finely sliced.
A skin of salt.
More beans.
Layered like sedimentary rock,
summer's glut becomes winter's bounty.

5. Rock Salt

The temperature falls.
Across midnight motorways,
through the 3-a.m. streets,
mechanical farmers sow the tarmac
with marled grain.

Angi Holden

SORTING

A neatly folded handkerchief,
the blue-embroidered "P" bold
against the weave;
a pen, a pencil, crushed receipts,
and in one pocket a single shell,
its sea-washed, thumb-worn edge
smooth as the years that slide beneath my touch.

Gravelines, an autumn day
and the wind gusting in from La Manche.
The children search the tideline,
bring whelk eggs and a mermaid's purse for your
    inspection.
And this shell, ridged grey and yellow
like the sunflower stubble burning in the fields,
its underbelly pink as your open palm.

Angela Topping

THREE WAYS OF SNOWDROPS

1.

They are just beginning to cast off
their pretence of being a bunch of grass,
nothing more nor less.

The snow came and buried them,
reigned silence for two days
before rain washed it all away.

It's as though they're still wearing
some icy drops of the stuff,
as though they kept a bit behind.

2.

Their folded hands commit
small white prayers
in the night's confessional.

Mea culpa, mea culpa, they say,
nun-like heads bowed
in the blankness of winter gardens.

3.

Now they congregate in little crowds,
slowly relaxing as the weather warms
and the garden remembers what it can do.

Joy Winkler

PRISON SCENES

Take a piece of satin, blue sheen,
appliqué to cool shadows
under a generosity of willow.
So many ducks this year.
You'll have your work cut out
to stitch them into the scene.
Whole families of them, squatting
on the green between prison houses.
Forty, fifty, more. Take a piece
of brown worsted, stitch
a mother duck, purposeful,
proud, her neck and head stiff
like an umbrella handle. Some
of the women rise early to feed them
on yesterday's sandwiches.
It's against the rules, but they know
mothers need encouragement,
need a little help along the way.
Take a piece of white thread,
stitch a discreet trail of breadcrumbs
leading away from the window.

***

In the hour's association time
they give their bodies up to sun,
some stick-straight, some
curved, coiled, clustered
on the embankment –
a reckoning in roman numerals,

21

a cyphered message
that can only be read from the moon.

***

Take a piece of silk thread,
spin it to a dull pallor,
scar it with snags,
pin it to a bed
in the shape of a woman.

Joy Winkler

PIECES

The picture squares to a prison house
built large with old bricks,
some dark red like gingerbread;
tall chimney, nice detail, just wide
enough for a small chimney-sweep.

The eaves dip neatly scalloped
to a row of curtsies. The roof's
edge is crenellated like a king's crown.
This is the place where Hansel
and Gretel once lived, before

they went off into the forest.
But now there's only Gretel,
who sits waiting for Cinderella's
footman to turn the great key in the lock
and pull up the drawbridge, well before

midnight. Moonlight floods
the Avenue, illuminates
the not-so-magical stepping
stones to the perimeter fence.
Old broken jigsaw-pieces lie

abandoned in the silver
handcuffs of snail trails.

Joy Winkler

KAMARIAH

for Kam, May 2006

Her name means "moon" –
her full name, her whole name,
part of herself that she has to hide.
She allows a thin nascent sickle,
or sometimes a quarter crescent.

Alone in the dark hours,
guarded by barred shadows
she shapes ink into words,
agitates memories, picks at old
scars until black blood flows.

Before dawn, she fingers
her night-loosed braids into tight
furrows, pulls her hood over
her bad dreams, believes
in the myth of an invisible cloak.

Gill McEvoy

RAIN DANCERS

Nothing in the taps but a choke of air,
cracks opening in our skin,
the pond shrunk to a dull bull's-eye
in a basin of mud, grass
shrivelled to bones and string.

In the night,
thrumming on slate, pooling in gaps,
hissing in gutters, slapping on stone,
whooshing down drains,
at last it comes.

As if a master-switch were thrown,
the lights go on,
heads bob at panes like dark balloons,

then people flood into the streets
to splash, and stamp, and roll
in wet. On the pavements

piles of nightclothes

rise

like river banks.

Gill McEvoy

EXERCISE IN THE MECHANICAL HORSE-WALKER

They're shut in this cage like museum exhibits.
Not threshing grain or powering a mill,
they are simply walking, round and round.

The cage turns, passing yet again
the big new house, wide lawns ungraced
by tree or shrub or flower-bed,

forcing them past fields – green leaps of freedom,
where they might kick and gallop, tails flying,
or buckle at the knees, roll over in the mud.

The fields turn, the stable yard, the garden.
The horses go on walking, heads hung low,
their tails down. Round. Round. Round.

Peter Branson

ON RED HILL

1.

This hill's a nub of legend; livestock died
mysteriously, witches conceived to meet.
In spring, high larks pulsed out their breathless strains
through spiral galaxing to paraglide
where lapwings wheeled to scream hysterically,
seasoned their ancient right to use the land.

A drovers' road once curled about the ridge
to source hill farms and far-from villages.
It's now a vague footprint and dwindles out
before the hidden ford below the falls.
Beneath an overwhelming limestone face,
once popular, long overgrown, tokens
of love are sealed in vaults of living stone.

2.

In olden times the people of the town
below the brow were sensible to moods
the weather tossed across the tall skyline.
Lore talked of violent August thunderstorms,
flash floods that kissed the eaves, and drownings too.
Once a blue moon or so, the stream that fed
mill-races, water-wheels, ground flour and bones
for china clay, recovered gravity,
rejigged its tired theme tune.
                                    Where iced winds bruised
through emptied starlit streets, few stirred beyond
warm hearth and candlewick, and false sunsets

behind the sombre overhanging crest
cast deepest shadow like a winding sheet,
dark reservoir that swamped all in its path.

3.

These days, few take the time to wander here,
the place where you rehearsed life's fingerprint,
mucked out and stabled bold forgotten dreams.
Over the years, new-fangled farmers' ways
and Stepford-like executive estates
have silenced larks, reeled in the peewits' dance.

In this brave cyber age – all wants and whims
mere credit cards away, our lives theme-parked,
folk stealing exercise on static bikes,
web-bound, stuck on "reality" TV –
the world has turned its back upon Red Hill.

Barbara Bentley

BURYING THE EVIDENCE

He torched the carcasses. He watched a herd
go up in flames when there was foot-and-mouth.
Years on, and another one's stiff in the barn,
poisoned by spine or spleen. Her brains
turned to sponge. Yet once she could jump the moon.

He daren't report it. And the knacker
wouldn't shift an infected corpse.
Nothing for it but to get rid in secret.
He'll wrap her up and dump her in a ditch,
as if she were a murder case.

His collie strains at the leash;
whines in the yard like a lone coyote
as his master lugs the burden onto the truck,
flings tarpaulin over haunches and hooves,
secures with a rope. It's all hushed up

till the engine revs. Diesel and dust as he moves
up the gears, squints through smashed flies.
Slow past the pub; under
the wires slung between pylons;
dipped lights through the Cheshire fields.

He does his best. But as he levers her
into a shallow grave, whisky unhinges
the way she was: how she swayed to the shed,
ears twitching and tagged for cash;
the steaming calf he'd pulled from her.

Far off, the Jodrell dish scoops up sky
and the teaspoon clink of distant galaxies.
A cat's cry is a bow on an untuned string.
It rings in his ears as he heads for home
where the moon, like a wife, waits up.

Frances Sackett

LETTERS TO MALTA

1. Child

The oak has been quiet since you left.
Almost May, and the woods are only just
Beginning with their stipple of leaf.

It will be summer before the threshing
Starts in the oak; the creak
And cranking of timber that netted

Your hands to your ears: *I'm the only one*
That sleeps at the back, you'd say,
If lightning strikes, if it falls, which way?

The wind that disturbs our oak is that
Same wind that brought you home from school
With all the seasons in your hair,

Aromas scenting your silkiness
With summer grass and autumn fires,
Frost blooming your skin to a russet apple.

There are beautiful words for winds,
The world is smaller for that,
Boreas, mistral, sirocco, simoom,

Recite them child –
Trade them back on the wind.

2. Daughter

It's here, you say,
Sixty miles south of Sicily,
A footprint north of the Libyan Desert;
In flying time it's negligible.

The airport is pushy
With pensioners off to their winter sun,
Disapproving of youth
With excess baggage –
The keepsakes and necessities
That vied for space;
The layers of clothing that
Still don't hide your slender frame.

Last hugs and kisses
Before you move to Departures.
No looking back,
But a turn to your partner –
A look that quivers with questions.

Then, as in the soaps,
When somebody says *Come with me*
And two characters disappear,
The smoked-glass doors of Passport Control
Conceal you.

Back at the house
The map on the floor:
MALTA. The word
Bigger than its boundaries,
An island smaller than my little fingernail,
Surrounded by sea and sea and sea.

3. Woman

Loss hangs about your room
Where the curtains stay open
And the night looks in
With its dark stare.

It paces the tidy bed,
Uncluttered tops of furniture.

But here you are rescued –
Here in these dried grasses
Filling a straight glass vase;
In the painted pottery jugs
Carefully placed on a pine shelf.

Your home is somewhere out at sea,
And each visit sees you
Trailing your cargo
In accurate weights
Over non-foetal waters.

You're "the English girl" now,
Hanging your washing on the roof,
Learning to live with the harsh sun.

At night, when you watch it sink
And turn the tiered rock to rose,
You might sometimes hear me call
I miss you –

Or, as you run to the roof
To watch fireworks,
Catch the glint of the moon
And feel its pull inside you,

Remembering how it insidiously
Pulled us together each month.

4. *Angel*

You would be the first to admit
You've never been an angel. But after
Our first visit, when the photographs
Had been developed, there you were
In the courtyard of the Grand Master's Palace,
Standing under a stone eagle,
Its long neck and beak
Crowning your head, its large wings
Perfectly placed and symmetrical,
Mysteriously giving you properties of flight,
Even in wings of stone.

5. *Balcony*

You know how a woman in Valletta will lean
From her balcony and call across streets
To another woman, and although she cannot see
The person she is calling, she hears answer
And is satisfied:
That is how I call to you now.

Rob Blaney

FIGUREHEAD

In 1865 the schooner Elizabeth Fry *foundered and sank near Yell, Shetland. Her figurehead washed up in Norfolk, her birthplace.*

Deliverance borne by the kiss of God,
she's home, clasping the good book to her chest,
her second coming up a Norfolk beach,
a worn-out stem of East India teak
snapped in a gale on a cape called Yell.
Elizabeth Fry, eyes shut, mouth wide open
as if to launch a damning sermon to
garner deathbed conversions, redeem souls.
An outstretched arm trails a flag of seaweed.
Her stiff upper lip quivers, seeps a groan,
ebbs back, forth, as if preaching revival.
Urging freedom for old lags, she rises up,
spits salt, and wags a splintered finger at
the last convict ship to Botany Bay.

Rob Blaney

RATION

Buckets to catch rainwater rust in the sun,
but after thunder it's tipping down
until leaks whet the tongue of the valley
and dribble through the kitchen roof.

Three years in desert war,
his morning shave is a scrape
over sandpaper skin.
It's an unchanged ritual:
no tap running or basin brimming,
he stoops camel-necked,
dabs a cutthroat into a cup,
mows stripes on his face,
flannels cheeks, staunches blood with soap.

He used to pay water-carriers
to bring flagons from cool springs,
sipping them in the lemon-scented shade
while the charged Nile dredged amber silt.
How he longed to swim again
in an English mere, catch frogs,
let them slip back with a plop into green gauze.

He polishes the unused sink,
stretches a hand outside, gargles,
and sings praises to the rain.
I wait for my bath, rapping on the door,
the tap trickling
as he rations my water ankle-deep.

The storm hammers on frosted glass.

Rita Ray

A PASSING-THROUGH ROOM

Nothing matches, but it's all good.
Worn grain tells of sometime ownership;
now no one stays long enough
to fill the chests and cabinets.
Those chair backs were carved to embrace;
legs curve aslant, enticing me to relax.

The veneer on the dresser has a golden edge,
leading the eye across a line of leaves.
Brass handles dangle from flower shapes.
A leather-framed blotting sheet lies unused
on the desk: handy mat for the laptop.
Insomnia seeps through the anaglypta.

At 3 a.m. you're listening to the World Service,
walking aimlessly around the room
opening and shutting empty drawers
as if to put things in,
longing to comfort them,
to help them bear their barrenness.

George Horsman

SUMMER MADNESS

Soon as the river watch moves on, they scramble
like rabbits from their hide in the old mill,
writhe over the spiked railing
and race for the weir. Thorn trees and brambles
are no bar, nor the black-skull sign:
Danger of Death. No Bathing.

The weir's a streaming spit. Upstream, dark depths;
below, a green weed-slithering slide.
Cormorants scatter as one tyke
in wrinkle-clinging jeans enacts his death,
falling, nose held, an arm spread wide,
where bureaucratic swans inspect the dyke.

Mad whoops and shrieks. A stripped lad, rapturous,
     plashes
the salmon ladder; another tightrope-dithers
along the bar, toes gripped into its grooves.
And as wet shanks and giddying sunlight clash,
I ask – as of night trains that slide by – whether
they're mad or I: does bank or river move?

Ruth A. Symes

HOME FROM HOSPITAL

Five weeks in hospital that time
Left you, to your surprise,
With a body half its normal size
And a house you did not recognise.

You struggled then from bed to chair,
Found alien all the places where
For years you'd entertained, washed up,
Made model railways and rung friends.

I remembered how once, when I was young,
You laughed and whooped as Uncle swung
Me upside down, and carried me around
That house. And how I laughed

To see the world made daft. I shouted then to you
How everything seemed strange and new,
How steps reared up at thresholds to the doors
And ceiling roses graced the floors.

Tonia Bevins

KISSES

From the first one, the alpha –
a winter flame snatched from the air
of an icy Esso forecourt

driving to the coast that Christmas –
the way ahead never seemed so clear.
I knew we would play the stars

through the passion, the sudden flare,
the fire catching hold, the laths beneath the mattress split,
the desultory late-for-work excuses,

through the absent-minded middle-passage years,
the settlement of flesh, the comfortable fit,
the counterbalance, the slow burn,

to the last one, the omega,
the screens pulled round
your lips so cold.